LOOM
Magic Fun!

9 Awesome, Never-Before-Seen Designs for
an Amazing Rainbow of Projects

John McCann
&
Becky Thomas

Scholastic Inc.

Visit our website at www.skyponypress.com.

Published by Scholastic Inc., 557 Broadway, New York, NY 10012, by arrangement with Skyhorse Publishing, Inc. SCHOLASTIC and associated logos are trademarks and/or registered trademarks of Scholastic Inc.

12 11 10 9 8 7 6 5 4 3   14 15 16 17 18/0

ISBN 978-0-545-72426-5

Printed in the U.S.A.   40

First Scholastic printing, February 2014

CONTENTS

ACKNOWLEDGMENTS

We would like to give many thank-yous to Kelsie Besaw, our champion editor, and to everyone at Skyhorse who worked with remarkable speed on this project. Thank you to Bill Wolfsthal, Tony Lyons, and Linda Biagi for putting this project together. Special thanks to Allan Penn, for your great photography and creative coaching, as well as to Holly Schmidt, for keeping us on track and making delicious sandwiches, and Monica Sweeney, for making sure everything made sense.

Our enormous gratitude goes to Jax Kordes as well as Olivia Sahagian for contributing such wonderful and unique projects to this book. Your ideas made this book extra special!

To all of the wonderful faces of *Loom Magic!*: Thank you Lucy Bartlett, Sally Brunelle, Quisi Cohen, Charlotte Penn, Noah Rotner, and Caleb and Owen Schmidt. This book would not be the same without you!

OCTO BRACELET

This pattern uses eight bands to make a repeating circle shape: that's why it's called "octo"! Or maybe it's because you'll want to make at least eight bracelets with this fun new stitch!

You need:

1 loom • hook • c-clip
49 rubber bands

1. Set up the loom with three rows of pegs, with the middle row set forward one peg (toward you). Loop a rubber band over the middle peg closest to you, then connect it to the peg one up and to the left. Loop another band around this peg and connect it to the peg above it. Loop one band around the peg you ended on, and connect it to the third middle peg. Start at the middle peg closest to you. Loop a band around this peg and connect it to the next peg up and to the right. Finish the rest of the circle as you did with the pegs on the left.

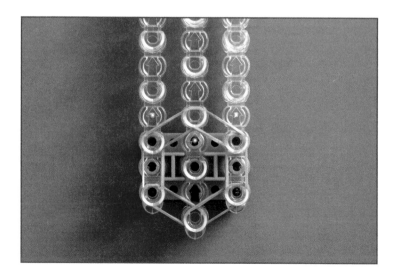

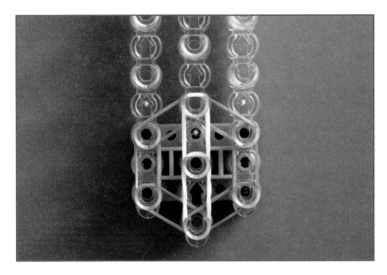

2. Loop a band around the middle peg closest to you, and connect it to the middle peg above it. Repeat with the next peg up.

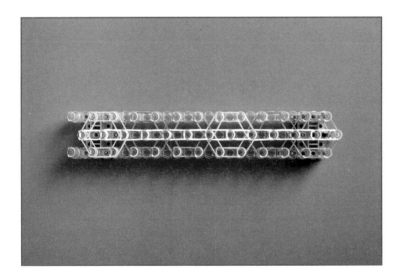

3. Starting on the middle peg three pegs up the loom, repeat steps 1–2, looping the left half of the circle, then the right, then looping the pegs up the middle. Continue up the loom, making 6 total circles. Loop one band around the middle peg furthest from you, then connect it to the peg up and to the right.

4. Turn the loom around so that the arrow is pointing toward you. Starting with the peg closest to you on the right, hook the second loop down on the peg, and pull it up and off the peg, looping it back onto the peg where the other end is still looped. Continue looping the rest of the pegs

in the same way, working your way up the loom. When you have looped all the rubber bands back onto their starting pegs, turn the loom again so that the arrow is facing away from you, and find the first peg you looped. Use your hook to grab all of the bands on this peg, and loop another band through these bands and pull it tight. You can also use a c-clip for this.

5. Remove the bracelet from the loom. Connect the two ends with a c-clip.

STRAiGHTAWAY BRACELET

This unique design will wow your friends, and it's a breeze to make! It will fit right in with the stack of bracelets on your arm!

> **You need:**
>
> 1 loom • hook
> 36 rubber bands

1. Set up the loom with the red arrow pointing away from you and the middle row set one peg closer to you. Loop a band over the middle peg closest to you, then connect it to the next peg up and to the left. Loop another band over this second peg, and connect it to the peg above. Continue to double loop in this way all the way up the left side of the loom. Do the same on the right side of the loom.

2. Loop one band over the last peg in the row on the left, and connect it to the last peg in the middle row. Do the same with the last peg on the right.

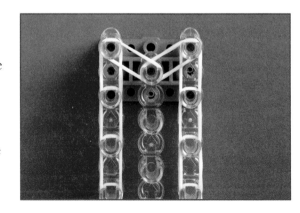

3. Loop a band over the first middle peg, and connect it to the middle peg above it. Loop a band over the closest peg on the left, and connect it to the second middle peg (where you ended your last loop). Loop another band over the closest peg on the right, and connect it to the second middle peg.

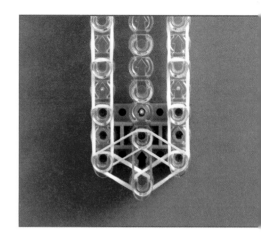

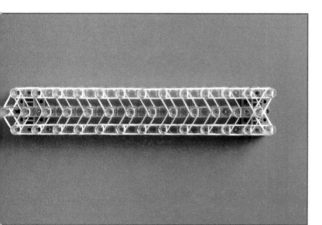

4. Move up to the second middle peg on the loom, and repeat step 3. Continue up the loom in this way until you reach the end.

5. Double-loop a rubber band and put it on the top middle peg.

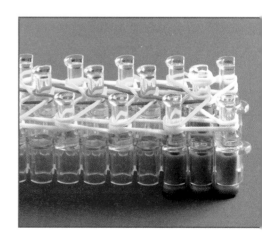

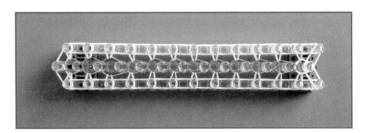

6. Turn the loom around so that the arrow is pointing toward you. Starting with the second middle peg, hook the second band on the peg and pull it up and off, looping back onto the peg where it started. Continue looping up the middle of the loom.

7. Start at the middle peg closest to you. Loop the edges in the same way. Loop the bands off this peg and back onto the first pegs on the left and right. Loop in the same way all the way up the left and right of the loom.

8. Remove your bracelet from the loom.

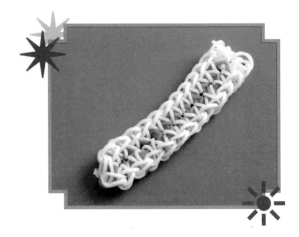

PiNNACLE BRACELET

This pattern is made by repeating a triangle shape all the way up the loom. It comes together quick, and it's sure to be a favorite!

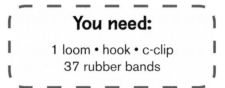

You need:

1 loom • hook • c-clip
37 rubber bands

1. Set up your loom with three rows of pegs set up squarely. Loop a band around the peg closest to you on the right, and connect it to the closest peg on the left (connecting all three pegs in the row). Loop a band around the closest peg on the right, then connect it up to the middle peg in the next row. Do the same with the closest peg on the left.

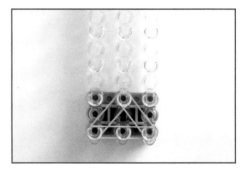

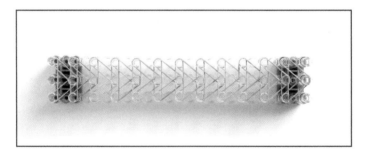

2. Starting on the right peg in the second row, repeat the pattern you made in step 1. Continue until you reach the end of the loom.

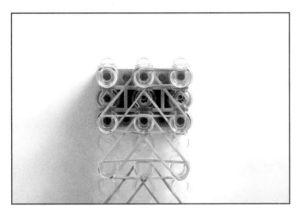

3. Loop a band around the middle peg in the last row, and connect it to the next peg to the right.

4. Turn the loom so the arrow is facing you. Starting with the middle peg, hook the second band from the top and pull it up and off, looping it back to the peg where it started. Move to the next row of pegs, and loop the bands from the corner pegs of the triangle onto the center peg in the same row. Continue looping this way until you've finished the loom.

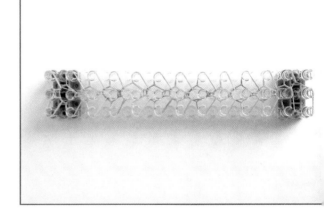

5. Secure the loops from the final peg with a c-clip, and remove your project from the loom.

SQUiSHY POOF BALL

This squishy poof ball is so much fun, you won't want to make just one. You can stick these cool little poof balls on your bracelets, your bike handlebars, or the zipper of your backpack, or you can toss them around with your friends! For even more fun, check out the Poof Ball Slingshot on page 19!

check out the Poof Ball Slingshot on page 19!

You need:

scissors • 1 loom • hook • c-clip
32 rubber bands

1. Set up your loom as shown, with two rows of pegs separated by an empty space between them.

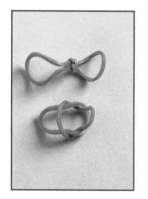

2. Take two rubber bands and tie them together. Repeat until you've used up all but two of the rubber bands.

3. Loop one of your tied rubber bands into the loom at an angle.

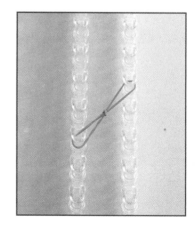

4. Take another tied rubber band and loop it into the loom at an opposite angle so the knots overlap and the bands make an X shape.

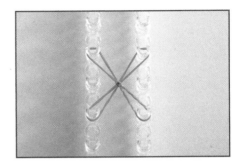

5. Repeat until you've used up all of your tied rubber bands.

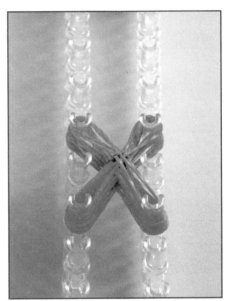

6. Loop one of your leftover rubber bands around your X from top to bottom. Pull one end through the other, and pull it tight.

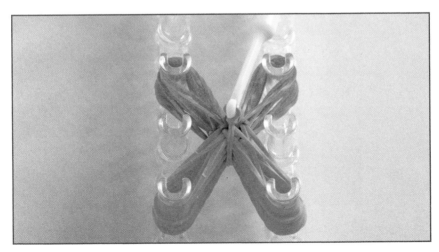

7. Secure the loop with a c-clip.

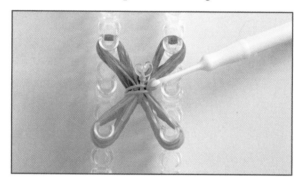

8. Loop your last rubber band around your X in the other direction (right to left), and pull it tight.

9. Hook the loop into the c-clip.

10. Remove your bands from the loom.

11. Cut through the loops at the end of your X. (Be careful not to cut the loops tied around the middle!)

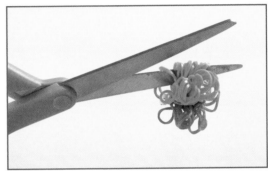

12. Fluff, squish, and squeeze your poof ball to make it round.

Notes: Stack more knotted rubber bands for an even bigger ball! You can also change up your color combinations to make different patterns.

POOF BALL
SLiNG SHOT

Ready, aim, fire! This slingshot project is quick and easy—make a bunch with your friends, then line up and see who can shoot the farthest!

You need:

1 loom • hook • 1 c-clips
36 rubber bands

1. Set up the loom with three rows of pegs lined up squarely. Turn the loom so the arrow is facing away from you. Loop a band around the bottom left peg, and connect it to the peg above it. Continue to double loop up the left side of the loom, ending on the fifth peg from you. Do the same on the right side of the loom.

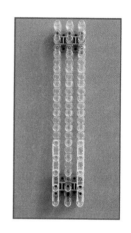

2. Loop a band around the middle fifth peg (right between your columns) and connect it to the peg below and to the left. Loop a second band around the middle peg and connect it to the peg below and to the right. Loop a band to the left peg in the fifth row, then connect it to the center peg in the row. Connect the center peg to the peg on the right.

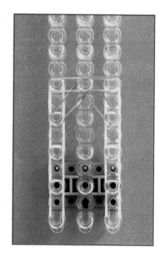

3. Connect the left peg in the fifth row to the peg above it. Do the same on the right side. Loop another band around the fifth peg on the left, and connect to the middle peg in the sixth row, up and to the right. Loop a band around the middle peg in the fifth row, and connect this to the middle peg in the sixth row. Connect the fifth peg on the right in the same way.

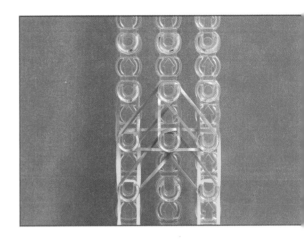

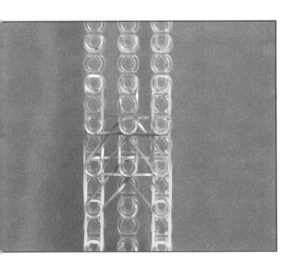

4. Loop a band around the sixth peg on the left and connect it to the middle peg in the row. Connect the middle peg to the peg on the right. Loop another band on the sixth peg on the left, and connect it to the peg above. Connect the middle peg in the sixth row to the peg above it. Connect the sixth peg on the right to the peg above it.

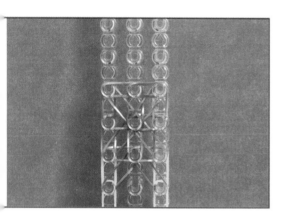

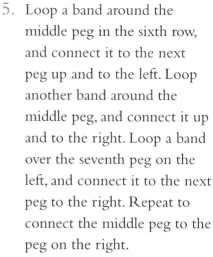

5. Loop a band around the middle peg in the sixth row, and connect it to the next peg up and to the left. Loop another band around the middle peg, and connect it up and to the right. Loop a band over the seventh peg on the left, and connect it to the next peg to the right. Repeat to connect the middle peg to the peg on the right.

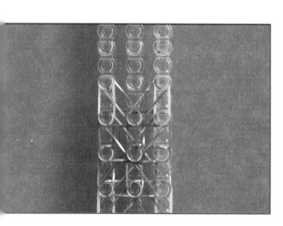

6. Connect the seventh peg on the left to the next peg above it. Do the same on the right side. Loop a band around the middle peg in the seventh row, and connect it to the peg up and to the left. Loop another band around the middle peg and connect it up and to the right.

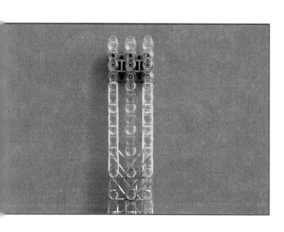

7. Starting on the eighth peg from you on the left, loop a band around the peg, and connect it to the peg above it. Repeat twice more to make a column of three bands. Do the same on the right side of the loom.

8. Turn your loom around so the arrow points toward you. Starting with the fourth peg from you on the left, hook the second band on the peg and pull it up and off, looping it back onto the peg where it started. Do the same with the next three pegs, then repeat on the right. Then loop the diagonal bands in the seventh row back onto the center peg. In the next two rows, loop the diagonal bands onto the center pegs, the horizontal bands from left to right, and then the vertical bands from the bottom to the top. Loop the bands on the center peg back to the pegs they came from. Start with the highest non-looped band, then work down until all bands are looped. In this same row, loop the bands on the right and left pegs to the pegs above them. From the center peg in the next row, loop all non-looped bands back to the peg they started on. Starting on the right and left in this same row, loop the bands back up to the peg above it. Continue looping the right and left columns in the same way until you reach the other end of the loom.

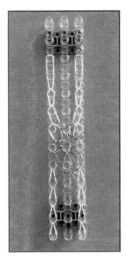

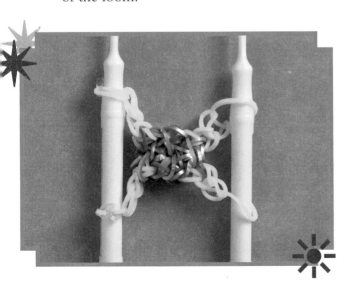

9. Remove your sling shot from the loom.

PEACE SIGN

Peace, love, and magic looms! This far-out peace sign comes together quickly and looks cool hanging in your window or on your wall!

1. Set up the loom with the middle column set one peg closer to you and with the arrow pointing away from you. Loop a band around the first middle peg, and connect it to the next peg above it. Repeat until you reach the end of the loom.

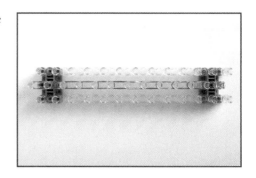

2. Loop a band around the first peg on the left, and connect it to the next peg above it. Repeat for five total bands. Do the same on the right side.

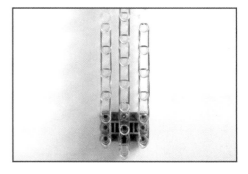

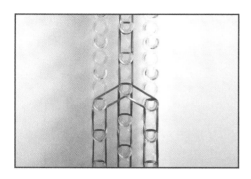

3. Loop a band around the sixth peg on the left side, and connect it to the peg up one and to the right. Loop a band around the sixth peg on the right, and connect it to the same middle peg.

4. Turn the loom around and, starting with the peg closest to you, pull the second band on each peg up and off, looping it back onto the peg where the other end is looped. Continue until you reach the end of the loom.

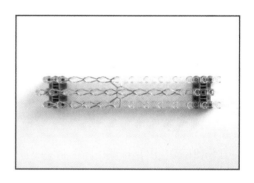

5. Pull your bands from the loom, and stretch them over your craft hoop.

6. Turn your loom so the arrow is pointing away from you. Loop a band around the first middle peg, and connect it to the peg up and to the left. Loop a band around the peg you ended on and connect it up and to the right. Continue this zigzag pattern until you reach the end of the loom.

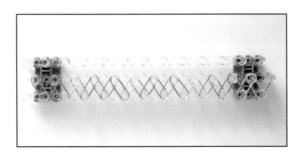

7. Lay your craft hoop over your zigzag pattern. Starting at the second looped peg on the end, hook the second band on the peg and pull it up and off, looping it over the craft hoop and back onto the peg

where the other end of the band is looped. Continue looping in this way all the way down the loom. As the bands are looped, pull them from the loom. Use a c-clip to secure the final band, or leave your hook on the loop to keep it from unraveling. Lay out your zigzag pattern again. Remove the c-clip from the band on the craft hoop and slide both ends of the band onto the top middle peg of your zigzag. Starting on this peg, loop the bands on your loom over the craft hoop and back onto their starting pegs as you did before.

8. Repeat steps 6 and 7 until you have covered your craft hoop. Secure the final loop with a c–clip, then connect it to the starting loop on the loom.

PENCIL TOPPER

Make writing and drawing even more fun by giving your pencils some extra flair! This pencil topper is super easy to make and can fit over your pencils and pens or can be made into a key ring for even more loom entertainment!

You need:

1 loom • hook • 36 rubber bands

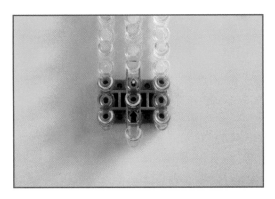

1. Start with the loom offset with the center pegs closer to you and the arrow pointing away. Loop a band over the first middle peg, and connect it to the third peg up.

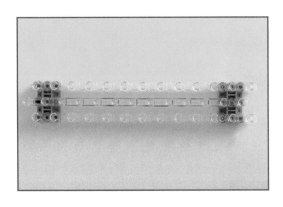

2. Loop a band around the next peg up, and connect it to the third peg above it. Continue looping the middle pegs this way all the way up the loom, until there is one empty peg left at the top of the loom.

3. Loop a band over the middle peg where you ended your last band, and connect it to the peg below it.

4. Loop a band around the second to last peg in the middle column, and connect it to the peg up and to the left. Loop another band around the second middle peg, and connect it to the next peg up. Loop another band around the second middle peg, and connect it to the next peg up and to the right.

5. Repeat step 4 until you cannot fit any more bands on the peg. This example uses twenty-four total bands, eight for each peg.

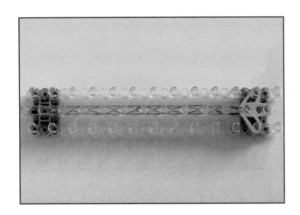

6. Starting at the second middle peg from the end (where you stacked all of the bands for the charm), loop the bottom band (the green band here) and pull it off the peg, looping it back onto the peg where it started. Continue looping this way as you work your way down the loom back to where you started.

7. Slide your pencil through the bands on the second peg, and then remove your project from the loom!

TRIPLE-OCTO SHOELACE CHARMS

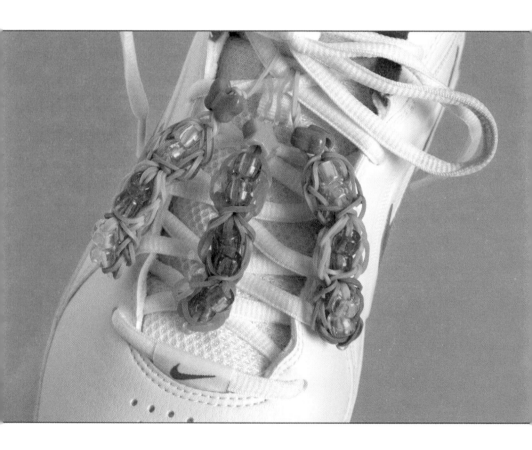

Make your kicks twice as cool with these Triple-Octo Shoelace Charms! You can customize them with different beads and colors to suit your style.

1. Set up your loom with the center pegs closer to you and the arrow pointing away from you. Starting on the center peg closest to you, do one Octo stitch: loop three bands around to make the left side of the hexagon, then start at the first center peg and do the same on the right side. Thread a band through a bead, and attach it to the first and second middle peg. Thread another band through a bead and attach it to the second and third middle pegs.

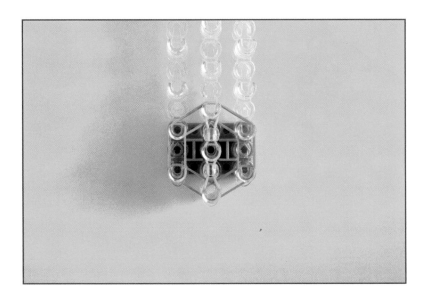

2. Starting on the middle peg where you ended your last Octo, do two more Octo stitches in the same way. Thread a band through a bead, attach the band to the top middle peg in your last Octo, and then connect it to the next peg above it. Loop a band around that peg, and connect it to the peg above it.

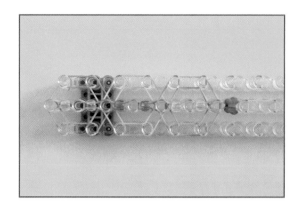

3. Turn the loom so the arrow points toward you. Starting with the looped pegs closest to you, loop the bands off the pegs and back onto the pegs where they began. Always hook the second unlooped band on the peg and loop it, looping all of the bands on a peg before moving on to the next peg. Loop all of the pegs in this way, working your way to the end of the loom.

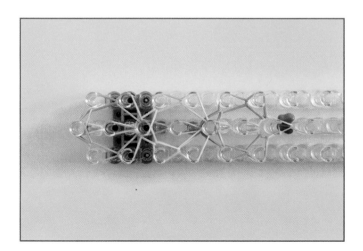

4. Secure the loose bands on the final peg with a c-clip or tie it off with another rubber band. Remove your charm from the loom.

5. Make two more Triple-Octo charms in the same way. Hook all the end loops together with a c-clip and attach to your shoelaces!

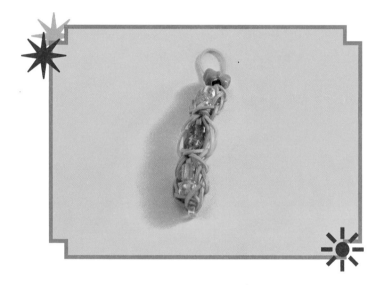

BLiNG RiNG

Don't settle for a plain ring; go big and make a bling ring! This beautiful piece of jewelry combines a ring and a bracelet—it's fit for a fashionista!

To Make the Stone:

1. Set up your loom with the middle pegs pulled closer to you and the arrow pointing away from you. Loop a band around the first middle peg, and connect it to the peg above it. Loop a band around the fourth middle peg, and connect it to the peg above it. Starting at the second middle peg, loop your bands to the left to make the first half of a hexagon, finishing on the fourth middle peg. Start again on the second middle peg, and loop your bands to the right in the same way to finish off your hexagon.

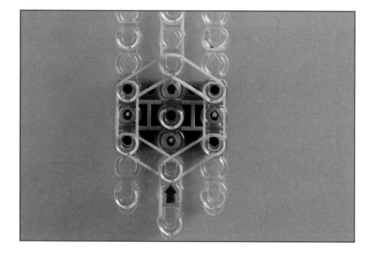

2. To make the spokes that will feature the beads, thread six bands with your six beads. With the first beaded band, loop it around the third middle peg (in the center of your hexagon), and connect it to the peg up and to the right. Continue to connect all six of the outer pegs with the beaded bands in this

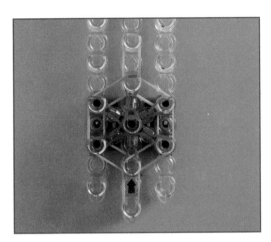

way, moving clockwise around the hexagon. Triple-loop a band on the middle peg of your hexagon as a cap band. Triple-loop another band on the fourth middle peg (the top of your hexagon) as another cap band.

3. Turn the loom around so the arrow is facing toward you. Start looping the bands of your spokes back onto the pegs where they started: First, loop the bands from the center of the hexagon, starting with the first band under the cap band, then loop counterclockwise around your hexagon. Next, loop the outer bands, starting from the left half and then the right in the same way that you placed the bands in the very first step.

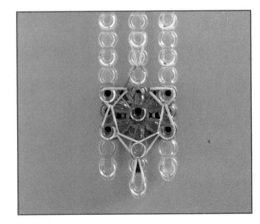

4. Loop the last band back to the last remaining peg. Attach a c-clip to secure the loose bands on either end, and then remove your project from the loom. Connect the c-clipped bands to make your ring band: loop several bands through one another to extend the band if it is too small.

To Make the Bracelet:

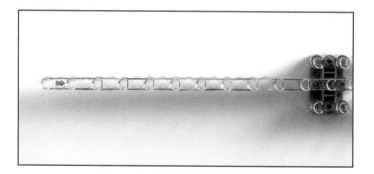

You need:

1 loom • hook
c-clip • 50 bands

1. Lay your loom horizontally with the arrow pointing to your right. Move the middle row all the way down and attach it to the loom on the second-to-last peg, so that it looks like a big

letter Y. Starting with the bottom of the Y, loop your first color from the first peg to the third peg (skipping the second peg). Loop your second color from the second peg to the fourth peg (skipping the third peg). Loop your third color from the third peg to the fifth peg (skipping the fourth peg). Repeat this pattern until you have reached the end of the row.

2. Now that you are at the base of the loom, loop a band from the second middle peg (the one that is next to last in the row) around the peg above it *and* the peg up and to the left of that peg (it will be the third peg in the first row). The loop will appear triangular. Loop another band from the same middle peg around the one above it and the one up and to the right (the third peg in the third row). The loop will appear triangular in the opposite direction. From the last peg in the middle row, loop a band around the peg up and to the left *and* the peg just above that one (the fourth peg in the first row). This loop will also appear triangular. From the last peg in the middle row, loop a band around the peg up and to the right *and* the peg just above that one as well (the fourth peg in the third row). This loop will appear triangular.

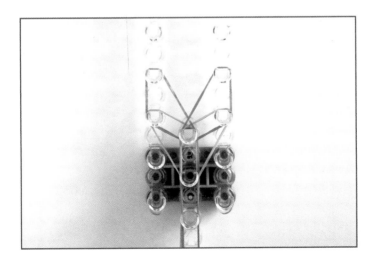

3. Like you did with the "tail," loop your bands down both outside rows, 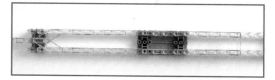 starting from the third peg and stopping at the twenty-first peg, making sure that each band is looped across three pegs instead of two. Connect the last two pegs on both sides with a band to close the rectangle-shaped side on the loom.

4. Starting with the very end of the loom where you closed off the rectangle, work 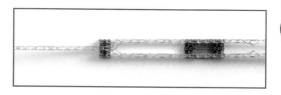 backward and hook the bands back onto the pegs where they started. This means that each band will skip a peg, just as it did when you first placed it down.

5. Secure the loose loops on the final peg with a c-clip. Carefully remove the project from the loom. Attach the end with the c-clip to the underside of the stone to complete your bling ring!